Traveling in space

Have you ever noticed how big the world is? If you could see it from a spaceship, it would look like a huge ball floating in space. And this is where we live—a planet full of animals, plants, and boys and girls like you.

But we are so small you wouldn't see us from out there!

2

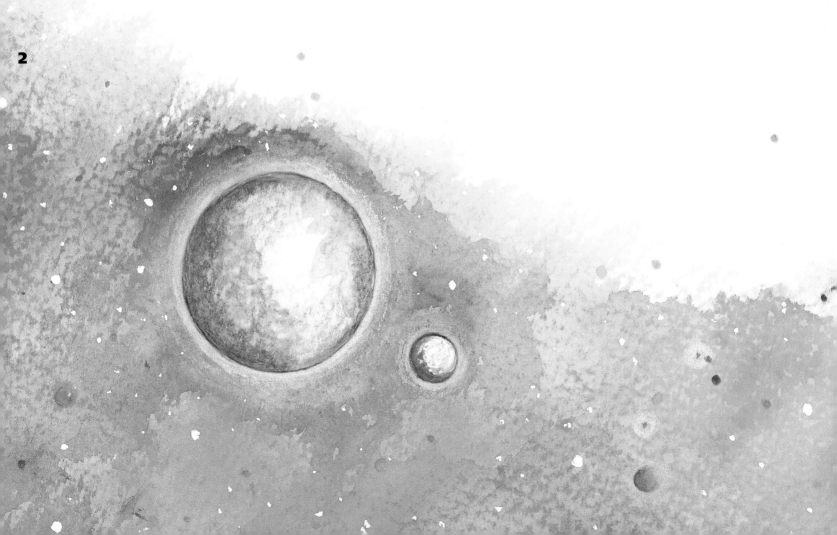

Would you like to travel around the world to see how boys and girls live from one end to the other? Imagine living in the desert, in the jungle, on an island, in a big city. There are so many different places!

3

What a lot of people!

There are millions and millions of people in the world, but among so many people, each one of us is different and unique.

The shape of your nose is different, and so are your eyes, the color of your hair, your skin, your height... Can you think of other characteristics?

A changing planet

The earth is so big that places on it are quite different from each other. There are very high mountains, jungles, deserts, rivers, and huge oceans.
People in those places have learned to live as comfortably as they can.

6

Everyone has his or her own habits and ways of dressing, speaking, and so on. It's a changing planet. What do you like best about the place where you live?

A celebration

Kai Li lives in a town in China. What she likes best is the celebration of the Chinese New Year, with the big dragon dancing and twisting along the streets. Kai Li helps decorate her home and cook special dishes for the visitors to her family. Those two weeks are lots of fun!

She gets hungry with so much celebrating and she loves eating fish with *mantou*, delicious Chinese rolls.

Long-distance school

Pall is an Inuit from North Alaska. It is extremely cold where he lives and school is far from home, so he attends an unusual school—during the coldest months, he studies at home, with the help of a computer and books he finds on the Internet.

When the weather is not so cold, he enjoys
riding his brother's snowmobile. It's very exciting!

11

Ichiro reaches the sky

Have you ever been in a big city? The buildings are so tall that some streets never get any sunshine. Ichiro lives in one of these big cities, Tokyo, in Japan. What he likes least of all is the noise from the cars. There are lots and lots of them everywhere.

His school is close, so he can walk there. What he likes best is learning to read and write, even when it is very difficult for him!

13

Draco

Draco is from Yugoslavia, where there was a war. One day, when he was walking to the market with his mom, a bomb fell near him, and now he has only one leg. He is all right now and he is happy the war is over and nobody else in his family was injured.

14

He feels sorry for the children who live in countries at war.

His biggest wish is for wars to disappear forever.

15

Living in the desert

Kadi lives in the desert of Namibia,
in Africa, in a hut made of cow dung.

A desert is a place where there is very little rain, and that's why Kadi and her people are nomads. It means they live in different places according to the seasons of the year, looking for places where there is grass for their goats and sheep. It is so hot there she does not need any clothes to keep warm, but she does like to wear bracelets. Kadi likes to look nice.

17

A musical branch

Tarita is an Australian aborigine. She lives in Sydney with her parents and grandparents and what she likes best is listening to her dad play the didgeridoo, which is a long, thin instrument. While he plays, she keeps dancing around him.

Her grandpa, when he was little, used to live in the Australian outback, where he hunted with a boomerang, which is a curved throwing club that returns to the thrower if it finds no obstacle in its way. Tarita wants to learn how to throw the boomerang, too!

Nawal

Nawal lives in a small town in Egypt. She gets up very early in the morning because she has to pick jasmine flowers with her two brothers. The money they get selling the flowers helps the family get along.

When they come back from the fields, they go to school. When she grows up, she would like to be a doctor so she can help heal people.

21

A city of water

Gina's dad works in a museum, which is a place full of pictures. They live in Venice, Italy, a very pretty city, full of old and beautiful buildings. The unusual thing about this city is that the streets are actually water canals!

To go from one place to another, people have to use boats. There are a few streets and squares, but they are often flooded and people have to wear rubber boots for protection. Gina loves it!

23

What a lot of trees!

Kinu lives in the Amazon jungle with all his tribe. His elders teach him the use of the different kinds of plants that surround them and which animals are good for food and which are poisonous, like some snakes and frogs.

The plants and the trees are so tall there that when it rains he hears the noise of the raindrops falling on the leaves, but he doesn't get wet because it is as if he were under a giant umbrella.

25

Living in the world

Have you ever been to a circus? If you have, maybe you went to Pol's circus. His parents are tightrope walkers and he has already started to try it. He loves living in a circus, always visiting new towns and cities. For him, the whole world is his home.

There are ten kids in the circus, from eleven years to three months old. The school-age children share the same teacher, whose name is Esther. Going to school in the circus is a lot of fun, but it's also a lot of work!

27

All different, all equal

There are people from one end of the world to the other. Some people are very old, like your grandparents, others are grown-ups, like your mom and dad, and of course there are children like you. Children all over the world like the same thing: having fun with family and friends.

28

○ ALASKA

○ BRAZIL

○ EGYPT

○ YUGOSLAVIA

We are not so different after all! Would you like to know more about people from all over the world? The way they speak, write, or dance, and so on? You have a whole world to discover!

29

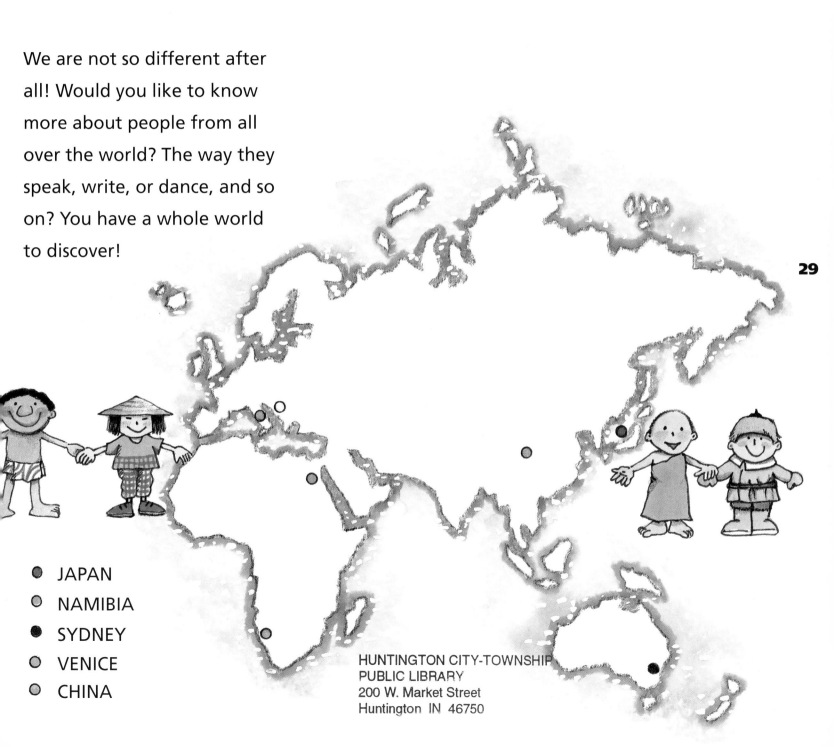

- JAPAN
- NAMIBIA
- SYDNEY
- VENICE
- CHINA

0   1   2   3   4

5   6   7   8   9

Numbers

Did you know you can say things using a whistle? You only need to agree with another person. For example, a long whistle means "Come here," two mean "I'm hungry," etc. If you want more people to understand your message, you will have to use a better-known system, such as the Morse code used by ships all over the world. Here is a list of numbers in Morse code: a dash means a long whistle and a dot a short one. Practice with your parents and soon you will be able to say numbers just using a whistle. Go ahead, try it!

An international language

There are many, many different languages in the world, so many in fact that it would be impossible to learn all of them. But you can make yourself understood even if you can't speak any other language but yours. You can try with your parents or friends. Imagine that you would like to ask them to give you something to eat. How would you manage without saying a word? And how would you indicate that you want to go to sleep? A more difficult choice: What would you do to make others understand that you are lost and don't know where your parents are? Now try it all alone; imagine something and do whatever you think necessary to make others guess what it is. Remember, you can't talk!

Cutout figures

Get a strip of color paper 20 inches (50 cm) long by 5 inches (12 cm) wide approximately. Draw a dotted line every 2 inches (5 cm) and fold the strip of paper on the dotted line, first to one side and next to the other. Draw half a silhouette as in the illustration, but be careful; both the arm and the leg must reach the edge of the paper. Hold the folded paper tight and cut out the figure very carefully. Color the eyes, the nose, and the mouth of every child forming the chain.

A game of the world

Almost everyone likes to play ball. If you are one of them, try playing this game from Portugal. You need only a soft ball and a few friends or relatives. All the players stand in a circle and pass the ball from one player to the next while counting 1, 2, 3, 4, and 5. The fifth player who gets the ball tosses it, trying to hit one of the other players who run away to avoid being hit. If the ball hits a person, this player is out of the game; otherwise, the player who threw the ball is out. The winner is the last remaining player. Good luck!

Guidelines for parents

Traveling in space

We can use this chance to explain how the earth rotates on its own axis while at the same time it moves around the sun. An easy way to do it is to represent both movements; the child is the sun and one of the parents moves around the boy or girl while rotating at the same time. You can get dizzy, but the child will surely understand the explanation!

With smaller children it can be done as a game. One child is called Earth and another is called Sun, but without trying to make them understand. As the children grow up, they start asking questions about the way things work and it is at this time that we will start giving them more detailed and deeper explanations.

34

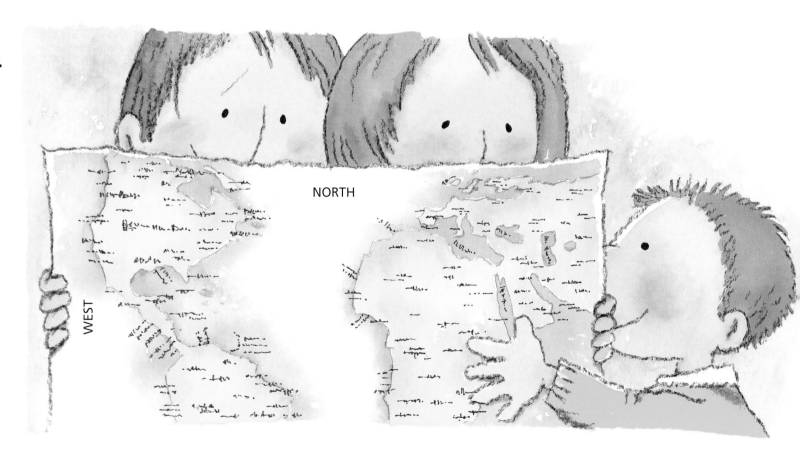

A celebration

This section mentions mantou, which are oriental rolls made of flour, sugar, and yeast. It is a good opportunity to tell the children about different food traditions. Some foods that are very normal for one country are considered very odd in other parts of the world, for example snails, snakes, sharks, horsemeat, worms, ants, and so on. It is important to make it clear that there is no food better than another, that it all depends on what people get used to eating since childhood and the kind of food available.

A musical branch

The didgeridoo is a musical instrument used by aborigine people in northern Australia. It is made out of a eucalyptus branch that termites have emptied out. It can be considered as a natural trumpet that you play applying your lips to it and blowing. There is a legend explaining the first sound made with a didgeridoo: There was a man picking up dried wood for the fire who found a branch full of termites. He blew to get the termites out of the branch so they wouldn't burn and that's the way the sound of a didgeridoo was heard for the first time.

Nawal

In many parts of the world, even in those countries that are called developed, there are many boys and girls who are forced to work to help the family income. In some cases it is pure child exploitation and the children work in conditions close to slavery. It is important to cooperate in the elimination of these practices by not buying products made using this kind of labor. At present there is a label with international recognition that indicates fair trade. It guarantees that no person, child or adult, has been exploited at any time in the manufacturing process.

Living in the desert

Deserts are characterized by the absence of rain and they can be hot or cold. As there is so little water in a desert, there are also very few plants. That's why people who live in the desert are usually nomads; when there is not enough food left for the animals, the whole group of people move to another place. If your children like looking at the map of the world, it is a good opportunity to talk about other desert people, such as the Tuaregs in the Sahara, the Bushmen in the Kalahari, or the Australian aborigines. All these nomadic peoples travel through the desert and have the ability to notice small marks in the landscape and remember them through generations.

35

What a lot of trees!

We can tell children that there are places in the world where it rains a lot, it is very hot, and there is thick vegetation. They are called jungles and are located around the equator. A great variety of plants and animals live in the jungle. In fact, there are so many that some of them are still unknown. Many medicines we use today include substances that originate in the jungle, and it is said that the cure for many illnesses will probably be found there.

All different, all equal

According to the ages of the children and their interests, we can tell them that besides the differences mentioned in the book there are many others, such as religion, music, dress, and so on, and that one is no better than the others; it's all according to custom. In the end, all children like the same thing—to live their childhood with enough of everything they need.

English language version published by Barron's
Educational Series, Inc., 2002

Original title of the book in Catalan:
**NENS I NENES DEL MÓN, D'UNA BANDA
A L'ALTRA**
© Copyright GEMSER PUBLICATIONS S.L., 2001
Barcelona, Spain (World Rights)
Author: Núria Roca
Illustrator: Rosa Maria Curto
Translation: Carlos Ganzinelli

All inquiries should be addressed to:
Barron's Educational Series, Inc.
250 Wireless Boulevard
Hauppauge, New York 11788
http://www.barronseduc.com

International Standard Book Number
0-7641-2141-3

Library of Congress Catalog Card No.
2001094052

Printed in Spain
9 8 7 6 5 4 3 2 1

Other titles of the series:

• *YOUR BODY, from head to toe*

• *YOUR FAMILY, from the youngest to the oldest*

• *FEELINGS, from sadness to happiness*

• *FRIENDSHIP, from your old friends to your new friends*

• *SCARED?, from fear to courage*